PSYCH
THERAPY

Healing Negative Emotions God's Way

TakeBackYourTemple.com

KIMBERLY TAYLOR

Table of Contents

Introduction

Do negative emotions threaten to overwhelm you? Through the power of God's word, they do not have to overcome you! Many of God's people are hurting today, but He has a promise and prescription to heal your hurt:

> "Then they cried out to the Lord in their trouble, And He saved them out of their distresses. He sent His word and healed them, And delivered them from their destructions (Psalm 107:20)."

I can testify that God's word heals. Over 10 years ago, I was nearly 100 pounds overweight. I felt defeated, depressed, and discouraged often. But God spoke to me in the midst of a chest pain: "It is not supposed to be this way."

I chose to believe His word and submit my heart to Him for healing. That is when my life starting changing.

Through seeing God at work in His word, I learned to recognize His work in my life. Today, He is not only my God, but my Father and Comforter of my soul. I walk with Him daily as His Holy Spirit leads and guides me.

I am no longer defeated, depressed, and discouraged, but am filled with His love, peace, and joy. Over time, I also stopped abusing food and achieved my ideal weight.

My prayer is that God's word transform you too as you read it, meditate on it and apply it.

Why God's Prescription Works

While God created you to experience emotions, there are Godly and ungodly ways to manage them.

Consider the word itself: e-motion. Emotions move you to action. Your emotions originate from your thoughts. You experience the fruit of

God's Spirit (love, joy, peace, patience, kindness, goodness, faithfulness, gentleness, and self-control) when you read, meditate, and act upon the truth in God's word.

Your goal is for God's word to become part of who you are.

John 8:31-32 explain this principle:

> "Then Jesus said to those Jews who believed Him, 'If you abide in My word, you are My disciples indeed. And you shall know the truth, and the truth shall make you free.'"

"Abide" means "live in" or "dwell." It does not mean a casual or passing visit. For example, you abide with a spouse and/or your children, however have a casual visit with coworkers or friends.

The difference is that you may like or even love your coworkers and friends, however you have a deeper relationship with family typically.

A healthy family relationship requires intimate knowledge and quality time spent together.
That is what I believe Jesus meant by abiding in His word.

A reward is built into living in God's word. Jesus promised that His word will make you free. Isn't freedom a sweet word? When I picture what freedom looks like, I see hands raised to the sky in praise and God's people singing to Him from the heart.

Unfortunately, that is not how most Christians live. Back when I accepted Jesus Christ as my Savior, I had no idea that there is victory in God's word. I thought that salvation was the end. I was happy that I wasn't going to hell!

So I went to church on Sunday and read the Bible during the church service. When church was over, I came home and put the Bible back on the shelf. "See you next week!"

I did not know about Romans 12:2:

> "And do not be conformed to this world, but be transformed by the renewing of your mind, that you may prove what is that good and acceptable and perfect will of God."

It would be great if your mind was renewed automatically when you accept Jesus as your Savior. But it is not. Renewing your mind requires diligent effort. Diligence means "consistent and careful attention." Whenever you see the value of something, you are willing to put time and effort into it.

Consider the often told story of Mary and Martha in the Bible:

> Now it happened as they went that He entered a certain village; and a certain woman named Martha welcomed Him into her house. And she had a sister called Mary, who also sat at Jesus' feet and heard His word. But Martha was distracted with much serving, and she approached Him and said, "Lord, do You not care that my sister has left me to serve alone? Therefore tell her to help me."

> And Jesus answered and said to her, "Martha, Martha, you are worried and troubled about many things. But one thing is needed, and Mary has chosen that good part, which will not be taken away from her (Luke 10:38-42)."

Many Christians are like Martha. They welcome Jesus into their house through saying the prayer of salvation. But that is where their story ends, like mine did. Their minds get pre- occupied with work, raising children, pursuing personal goals, or even ministry. They never let Jesus become part of their private world.

So Jesus remains just a common guest to them, not an honored member of their family.

In contrast, Jesus said that Mary **chose** the good part. Mary made a decision to sit at
Jesus' feet. She gave Him her
full attention. She treasured His word and wanted to hear what He had to say. According to Jesus, that is the good part of life!

Could it be that we are experiencing so much defeat, oppression, and depression in the body of Christ because many of us are not seeking after the good part?

In John 14:21-24, Jesus gives us a pattern for greater intimacy with Him:

He who has My commandments and keeps them, it is he who loves Me. And he who loves Me will be loved by My Father, and I will love him and manifest Myself to him.'

Judas (not Iscariot) said to Him, 'Lord, how is it that You will manifest Yourself to us, and not to the world?'

Jesus answered and said to him, 'If anyone loves Me, he will keep My word; and My Father will love him, and We will come to him and make Our home with him. He who does not love Me does not keep My words; and the word which you hear is not Mine but the Father's who sent Me.'"

The way to know the Lord at a deeper level is to hear the word, meditate on the word, and do the word. You are not doing this to
earn God's love; after all, you already have that. Rather, you obey His word **because you love Him**.

Loves comes first, then obedience, not the other way around! When you obey the Lord's word, it becomes part of who you are. By extension, so does He.

Because God's word has power to change your life, I hope you decide to put it into practice. As your mind is renewed, you will see your world change. After all, you've got the Healer living in your house now!

Weeding out Lying Thoughts

I've got a question for you: Have you ever heard of someone going out to plant weeds? Of course you haven't. Why? Because weeds spring up by default.

The world's way of thinking is the equivalent of mental weeds. Any thoughts that do not agree with God's word are lying thoughts.

That is what is happening with many Christians whose minds are not renewed. Because they think the way the world thinks, they feel the way the world feels, and act the way the world acts.

So the world sees little difference between Christians and themselves. Because they see us as oppressed as they are, they do not see a reason to serve our God!

Back to our garden analogy, think about a person who wants a pretty garden. What does it take to get one? It takes planting good seed, watering and fertilizing the ground that has been planted, and pulling up the weeds.

If you don't pull up those mental weeds (lying thoughts), then they have the potential to take over the garden!

I mentioned years ago that I suffered from depression. One thought driving that depression was that no one cared for me. While the feeling was true, it was based upon a lying thought. If I had not questioned it (and persistent thoughts like them), they would led me to suicide.

The enemy often sows lying thoughts into Christians' minds to steal, kill, and to destroy us. But Jesus came that we might have life. We can live in His peace when we develop His mind according to 2 Corinthians 10:5:

> "casting down arguments and every high thing that exalts itself against the knowledge of God, bringing every thought into captivity to the obedience of Christ…"

Because Jesus is the living Word, your goal is to assess your thoughts to ensure they agree with His word. Acknowledge your feelings but then ask yourself, "What must I believe to feel this way?" That will help you to uncover the thought behind the feeling and see if that thought agrees with God's word.

From my example, I believed that nobody cared for me. To take the thought captive to the obedience of Christ, the next question is important: Is this thought true?

If I only kept looking at my circumstances, I could say 'yes' because no one was around to comfort me. But human perception is limited. So I realized that I needed to look into God's word because His thoughts are higher than ours and so are His ways.

Looking at God's word in 1 Peter 5:7 told me why my thought was a lie: "casting all your care upon Him, for He cares for you." So that scripture told me that God cares!

So remember: Just because you feel an emotion does not mean the thought behind it is true. So to glorify the Lord with your actions and be healed of negative emotions, then ensure that your thoughts are based upon the truth in God's word. Freedom awaits you!

Therapy from the Book of Psalm

In this book, you are going to take a tour of some key chapters from the book of Psalm in the Bible. I don't think it is a coincidence that God followed the book of ultimate suffering in the Bible (Job), with the book of ultimate comfort (Psalm).

Whether you are struggling with feelings of abandonment, anger, anxiety, doubt, fear, or other negative emotion, you will find people to whom you can relate in the book of Psalm.

Now, a word of caution: Not everyone dealt with their emotions in Godly ways in the book of Psalm. Just because the Bible records what happened doesn't mean that it approved what happened!

So we'll examine each person's viewpoint to decide whether to "follow this example" or "don't do what this person did."

As you read each Psalm, I recommend you use the following questions to guide your meditation on the message:

- Whom is speaking?
- To whom are they speaking?
- Where is God?
- Where am I (can you relate to the person or their situation)?
- How does this apply to my life?

To get the most from this book, I also recommend the following:

• A Bible: I recommend the New King James Version or the New American Standard Bible for readability. I believe that it is important to use a Bible translation that you understand for private study.

In many Bibles, there is a topic listing at the back. In the listing, you can look up scriptures that relate to the emotion you are feeling.

Alternatively, you can also perform an Internet search for scriptures. For example, let's say that you are experiencing depression. You can look up "Bible depression" or "Bible joy" for scriptures that can help in your situation.

• Index cards: These will come in handy to write focus scriptures on so that you can 'feed' on them throughout the day.

• A small notebook or journal: This will enable you to keep track of the blessings/lessons you are learning. Personally, I use the website 750words.com as an online journal. It is free for 30 days and requires a small fee to use after that.

Most importantly of all, have a heart and mind that is open to the Holy Spirit's teaching. One of His roles in the believer's life is that of Teacher (John 14:26).

Before you start your study, I recommend you invite the Holy Spirit through prayer to minister to your heart. Ask Him to show you the lesson God wants to teach you plainly.

For added impact, I recommend reading this book out loud, especially if your heart is feeling heavy or overwhelmed. Hearing your own
voice speaking God's word can increase your faith.

Be attentive to the still small voice of the Holy Spirit that prompts you to take action on the word you are learning about.

As you apply God's word, you will learn how to manage your emotions according to God's ways!

Abandoned
Psalm 88

Focus Scripture: "O Lord, God of my salvation, I have cried out day and night before You. Let my prayer come before You; Incline Your ear to my cry (Psalm 88:1-2)."

I have been abandoned before. My father left my mother when I was just a baby. Even though my mother loved me, I spent a great part of my life with a painful question: Why didn't my father love me enough to stay?

So I can relate to Psalm 88 in which Heman the Ezrahite wrote about feeling as if he was abandoned. He felt despondent, as if there was no hope in his situation. He felt far from friends and family to care for him.

As you read the Psalm, you can feel his raw pain through the words he has chosen to use to describe his feelings. His word choice largely included those associated with death: *grave, pit, slain, depths*.

Psalm 88:8-9 summarizes the height of his despair: "You have put away my acquaintances far from me; you have made me an abomination to them; I am shut up, and I cannot get out; My eye wastes away because of affliction."

In this Psalm, the writer expresses his belief that God was responsible for his troubles. He felt as if God was nowhere to be found in his troubles and that God was angry with him.

Now the writer's words were true in that they truly expressed how he felt at the time. But were the thoughts behind those feelings true according God's word?

No, they were not.

Even though the writer felt like God had abandoned him, God's own word in Deuteronomy 31:6 says that He will never leave us nor forsake us. So even though the writer couldn't "feel" God with him, yet God was there because He promised He would be.

The question you must always ask yourself when you are feeling negative emotions is this: Will I believe my feelings above what God has said?

If you are feeling abandoned, it is okay to acknowledge that you feel that way, but follow up with a reality check. God's word promises His eternal presence. Feelings change all the
time which is why they can't be
trusted - especially if they are based
upon lying thoughts.

You are not alone. You are not abandoned. Some people may leave you but God never will. Comfort yourself through reminding yourself of the truth. God is with you, even during times of affliction. If God is for you then who or what can be against you?

Angry

Psalm 13

Focus Scripture: "But I have trusted in Your mercy; My heart shall rejoice in Your salvation. I will sing to the Lord, Because He has dealt bountifully with me (Psalm 13:5-6)."

A former manager made me angry once. I was already stressed from trying to write documentation for 3 products in development at the same time. It felt like trying to change a flat tire while the car was still in motion!

The deadline for completion was fast approaching and I knew the deadline would not be met. I told my manager this fact and why. Since the documentation for all products was due at the same time, I asked her which product was the priority.

She said, "Everything is a priority." And she was serious. She offered no solutions nor help.

That is when I got angry. I didn't say a word and left the building. I knew I needed to calm down or else I'd say something I'd regret. I had to walk around a fountain outside seven times to get control of my feelings, talking to the Lord the whole time.

Anger occurs when you feel like your rights have been violated or your expectations have not been met. In my case, I expected my manager to support and assist me during a tough situation, but she did not.

David in the Bible is an extreme example of someone whose rights had been violated. He had done nothing wrong, yet King Saul (his manager) was trying to kill him (see 1 Samuel 19).

A prophetic word was given to the prophet Samuel that God had chosen David as the new King. But the old king, Saul wanted to hang on to his throne, even though God had made it clear to him that the kingdom was no longer his.

So David was now on the run. He was denied the comfort and peace of home - all because of Saul, whom he had served faithfully. David felt angry, alone, and tired.

In the midst of His trouble, David called out to the Lord, wanting to know how long he had to suffer from that situation.

No record exists to tell us that David's inquiry was answered. And yet, after David expressed his painful feelings, he started reflecting on the Lord's goodness and mercy. He reflected on God's salvation because God had delivered him from the enemy's hands.

In the end, David said that he would sing to the Lord because the Lord had dealt bountifully with him. Bounty means plenty. So David recognized God as the source of his supply. He was dependent upon the Lord for his very life.

Why should the recognition of the Lord's generosity make David want to sing? Because even though the circumstances were
challenging, that did not change David's viewpoint of God.

Plus, scripture says that God inhabits the praises of Israel (Psalm 22:3). By extension, this fact applies to us since we have been adopted
into God's family through our salvation in Jesus Christ.

To draw God closer to you, praise Him in the midst of whatever emotion you are feeling. He can give you the strength to love your enemies, bless those who curse you, and pray for those who spitefully use and persecute you. You don't do it to please man. You do it to please God, who is worthy to be praised!

Psalm 58

Focus Scripture: "So that men will say, "Surely there is a reward for the righteous; Surely He is God who judges in the earth (Psalm 58:11)."

Psalm 58 can be politely called, "David's rant against the wicked." When you read it, you can practically hear David's indignation about
people who wrong others. David's anger is perfectly natural as he describes the character and deeds of these people. However in verse 6, he takes a dark turn. David starts asking God to hurt wicked people physically!

I have read that certain pastors say that it is okay to pray for harm to come to your enemies. They call it "imprecatory prayer." But that is wrong and it contradicts what God tells us to do.

In Luke 9:51-56, a Samaritan village did not receive Jesus. When His disciples saw this, they asked Jesus if they should command that fire come down from heaven to consume them.

But Jesus said that they did not know what manner of spirit they were of. In Matthew 5:43-48, he tells us how to deal with enemies:

> "'You have heard that it was said, 'You shall love your neighbor and hate your enemy.' But I say to you, love your enemies, bless those who curse you, do good to those who hate you, and pray for those who spitefully use you and persecute you, that you may be sons of your Father in heaven.'"

In Ephesians 4:26, we are told "'Be angry, and do not sin': do not let the sun go down on your wrath…"

You might say, "Well, David didn't do anything; what could be the harm in wishing, hoping, or praying that your enemies be hurt?" Well, Jesus also taught that murders, adulteries, and other sins come from the heart.

We need to avoid allowing anger to take root in our hearts. One way you can do that is to forgive quickly. Forgiveness is not a suggestion but a command. Jesus says that if you don't forgive others, that our Father in heaven will not forgive you (see Matthew 6:14-15).

I read a statistic recently that over 60% of cancer patients have a problem with forgiving others. My pastor once said that unforgiveness is like drinking poison and hoping the other person will die.

So for your health's sake, forgive. Taking that step is easier when you recall how much Jesus has forgiven you. Since He released you from your sin debt, so you should release others from the debt you feel they owe you.

Remember that God words says that vengeance belongs to Him and that He shall repay (see Romans 12:19).

Trust in the Lord to mete out justice in His good time and in His sovereign way. Plus, you know your obedience will be rewarded. God's word says that it will and you must take God at His word.

Anxious

Psalm 23

Focus Scripture: "Yea, though I walk through the valley of the shadow of death, I will fear no evil; For You are with me; Your rod and Your staff, they comfort me (Psalm 23:4)."

When I read the 23rd Psalm, I am taken to a place of tranquility and peace instantly. My anxious thoughts quiet down at just the first sentence: "The Lord is my Shepherd." I love the image of God as my Keeper, Protector, and Deliverer. I am not alone. I have His Presence with me at every hour of the day.

Have confidence that the Lord makes you to lie down in green pastures, which means that He is taking you to a place of rest and stillness in

Him: "Be still and know that I am God (Psalm 46:10)."

If you are always running around and don't have quiet time with the Lord, then how can you receive restoration in your mind, will, and emotions? Modern life can drain you dry if you let it. That is why so many people are emotional wrecks. They are running on empty. But God promises to restore us.

Once you receive rest and restoration in the Lord, then you can walk with Him as He leads you into paths of righteousness. He shows you how to think right, believe right, and live right.

Even though your circumstances make you feel as if you are walking through Death Valley, you will not fear because you know the Lord is with you. God's goodness toward you will be so visible that even your enemies will see His handiwork upon your life. They will see God's grace abounding toward you.

What is God's grace? Grace is everything God is and has made available to you. In old movies about royalty, you see people addressing the King or Queen as "Your Grace" as they bow down. Jesus is "Your Grace." He gave His very life for you. In Him, you have a new identity as the beloved of God.

In Jesus, you have forgiveness of sin and victory over sin. In Him, you have peace and joy because He left you with both. In Him, you have love and with His love, you are empowered to love your neighbor as yourself.

When you consider this, then you see that material things cannot compare with the riches of His grace! Because Jesus is your Shepherd, then you indeed shall not want when you meditate on all that you have in Him.

Focus Scripture: "Rest in the Lord, and wait patiently for Him; Do not fret because of him who prospers in his way, Because of the man who brings wicked schemes to pass. Cease from anger, and forsake wrath; Do not fret—it only causes harm (Psalm 37:7-8)."

Psalm 37 deals with an age-old question: Why do the wicked seem to prosper? Why do the righteous struggle?

In the Psalm, David gives assurance that things are not as they seem. Ephesians 6:12 tells us that we don't wrestle against flesh and blood, but against principalities, against powers, against the rulers of the darkness of this age, against spiritual hosts of wickedness in heavenly places. So we are in a Spiritual battle.

Once you realize this, then you see that the enemy has no need to fight against wicked people. Since they are already his, why does he need to fight against his own?

But the enemy will fight against us; we are the ones praying for others, loving our neighbors as ourselves, and doing good works to glorify the Lord. Because we love the Lord, the devil hates us.

It is good to be on the Lord's side!

Yet, we can get discouraged when it appears the wicked have it easier than we do. But David encourages us in this Psalm. He is saying that even though we may be going through a difficult time, we have a wonderful reward waiting for us. And even though the wicked may be having an easier time now, God's judgment and justice awaits them - and it ain't going to be pretty!

So David is telling us that rather than be anxious about our current circumstances, to focus on living righteously before the Lord, knowing that we have an eternal heritage in Him. He gives us much familiar encouragement in this Psalm:

- "Delight yourself also in the Lord, And He shall give you the desires of your heart (verse 4)."
- "Commit your way to the Lord, Trust also in Him, And He shall bring it to pass (verse 5)."
- "The steps of a good man are ordered by the Lord, And He delights in his way (verse 23)."
- I have been young, and now am old; Yet I have not seen the righteous forsaken, Nor his descendants begging bread (verse 25)."

Whenever you are feeling anxious and think that you are laboring in vain, do not believe those lying thoughts! Instead, do what David recommended in the 4th and 5th verses.

Your heritage on the Earth is your right to seek the Lord's presence. You have full access to Him through your relationship with Jesus.

Because God has made His home with you, retreat to him whenever you are worried. Feed upon His faithfulness by remembering those times when He has come through for you. You need to do this because one of our human weaknesses is the tendency to forget.

To help yourself remember, I recommend that you keep a journal of testimony. You overcome by the blood of the Lamb (Jesus) and the word of your testimony (Revelation 12:11).

So whenever the Lord shows Himself strong on your behalf, then write down your testimony about what He has done for you. Then feed on that when you need it and praise the Lord for bringing you through.

Delight in your identity in Him. You are the son or daughter of the most High God. That is a position of honor. So sing and make melody in your heart to the Lord.

Maintain a focus on being thankful that you are in His kingdom and that you are fighting in God's righteous cause to save lost people. With that big picture view, then you know that you don't have a reason to be anxious. The Lord's got this!

Psalm73

> *Focus Scripture: "Whom have I in heaven but You? And there is none upon earth that I desire besides You. My flesh and my heart fail; But God is the strength of my heart and my portion forever (Psalm 73:25- 26)."*

I read a news story once about a famous R&B singing couple who "made it rain" in a nightclub, distributing almost $100,000 in one night upon the patrons. I admit I had a brief feeling of envy when I read that. Imagine having enough money to give away $100,000!

Then I recalled that same couple was in another news story because the husband got into a physical elevator brawl with his sister-in- law. His wife was standing by.

Can you put a price upon peace with your family? Peace is worth way more than
$100,000!

In the end, money will fade away like all the other material things on this Earth. The only thing that is eternal are our spirits. We are all going to live somewhere when our life on Earth is over. Aren't you thankful that you have
picked the Lord's side so that you can live in Eternity with Him?

I love Asaph's declaration in Psalm 73:1, "Truly the Lord is good to Israel!" Has the Lord been good to you? Scripture tells us that it is God's goodness that leads to repentance. Whenever you are in an anxious state and want to have a change of heart, then take a moment to meditate on how good God has been to you:

•   Do you have breath in your lungs? Praise God!

•   Do you have a roof over your head? Praise God!

•   Do you have clothes to wear? Praise God!

•   Do you have food to eat? Praise God!

•   Do you have shoes to put on your feet? Praise God!

God is the source of every good thing and He deserves to be praised.

Sometimes, like the Psalmist says, our flesh and our heart fail. But our Spirit man is revived when we realize that the Lord Himself is our strength and our portion forever. He is the one from whom we draw when we need refreshment and strength.

I can testify that drawing close to the Lord when I am anxious is like receiving a cool drink of water on a hot day. Oh how wonderful it is! Jesus is truly the Living Water and through the Holy Spirit, we don't have to thirst. His presence is always there!

So when your heart is overwhelmed, go to the Rock that is higher than you are. Ask the Lord to fill you up with His peace to overflowing.
With the Lord, you don't have to worry about portion control!

Fill yourself up with the Bread of Life. His word is our bread and within it is the power of God to salvation. It is a lamp unto our feet and a light unto our path. His word brings our strength, encouragement and wisdom. It
renews us to the Lord's thoughts and ways.

We have good words for our health, for our strength, for our encouragement, for our marriage, for our children, and for our finances. Do you need help in these areas? The wisest thing to do is get a word from the Lord about it. Hold on to that word, meditate upon it, and do what it tells you to do until your change comes.

Oh, thank the Lord for taking time to send us His word to heal us and deliver us from our destructions!

Discouraged

Psalm 42

---

*Focus Scripture: "Why are
you cast down, O my soul?
And why are you disquieted
within me?
Hope in God; For I shall yet
praise Him, The help of my
countenance and my God
(Psalm 42:11)."*

In Psalm 42, the sons of Korah wrote
about discouragement. Discouragement
means that your courage is taken away,
which can happen when the source of it is
misplaced.

When I am discouraged I often ask myself,
"Where is your hope?" I never fail to
recognize that I have placed my hope in
another person or circumstance during
those times. But the truth is that other
people can fail and

disappoint you; circumstances can change unfavorably. However, our God in heaven is the same yesterday, today, and forever.

I believe that during times of discouragement, your soul is really thirsty for God. That is when you need to re-connect with the source of your hope and courage, seeking the Lord's presence, studying the Word, prayer, praise, worship, singing Spiritual songs, and serving others for God's glory.

The sons of Korah knew how important it is to seek God's face continually. You can hear their longing for God in the question "When shall I come and appear before God?" You see, they did not have the indwelling Holy Spirit inside of them.

However when we accepted Jesus as our Savior, the Holy Spirit came to live inside of us. So we can go into the temple, into our innermost being, to meet with the Spirit of God right where we are. We have confidence that

when we hunger and thirst
after righteousness, we are
filled!

The sons of Korah knew the source of
encouragement: "Hope in God." When
you remember that your hope is in God,
not a person nor circumstance, it steadies
your soul and makes your countenance
brighter. In the Psalm, they speak of
remembering the Lord, His presence, His
power, His lovingkindness, and the song
He has placed in their hearts.

Although you may feel that the Lord has
forgotten you sometimes, He hasn't. This
is another situation in which your feelings
have to be measured against God's word.
Scripture records that the Lord has His
people engraved on the palms of His
hands (see Isaiah 49:16)! So we are with
Him permanently.

During times of discouragement, we must
always remember where our help comes
from. Our help comes from the Lord, who
made heaven, Earth, and us. As a result,
our

circumstances have to bow before Almighty God!

Doubtful

Psalm 119

---

*Focus scripture: "Remember
the word to Your servant,
Upon which You have caused
me to hope (Psalm 119)."*

Psalm 119 is the longest book in the Bible
and I don't think that is an accident. The
Psalmist writes about the delights and
benefits of abiding in God's word. The Lord
desires that His people become wise and
understanding.
Why? He wants us to stand out among
those who do not know Him. This can only
happen as we apply the wisdom and
understanding in
God's word:

"Surely I have taught you statutes and
judgments, just as the Lord my God
commanded me, that you should act
according

to them in the land which you go to possess. Therefore be careful to observe them; for this is your wisdom and your understanding in the sight of the peoples who will hear all these statutes, and say, 'Surely this great nation is a wise and understanding people (Deuteronomy 4:5-6).'"

As I read and meditate on the Psalm, several phrases pop out at me:

- "Teach me Your statutes"
- "I hope in Your word."
- "According to your word."

With the phrase "teach me Your statues," the Psalmist demonstrates that he has a teachable spirit and a desire to please the Lord. If he did not have a desire to learn, he wouldn't have asked for teaching. So he recognized his need for understanding and knowledge, knew the Lord was the source of understanding and knowledge, and humbled himself enough to ask.

This Psalm speaks of someone who wanted to know what the Lord required of him and to learn what it takes to live a righteous life. This is a man after God's own heart!

The next phrase "I hope in your word" is one in which the Psalmist tells us where his hope lies. His hope did not lie within himself, other people, nor his circumstance. He hoped in God's word because, although the things around us may change, God's word never changes! His character never changes.

We can hope in God's word because we hope in His character. We know that it is impossible for God to lie so if He said it, He will do it. If God spoke it, He will make it good. So our hope and confidence in times of doubt should always lie with God's word.

The reason why so many Christians are doubtful is because they either don't know what God's word says about a situation or they don't believe God's word.

When presented with God's word some say, "It may be true for them, but it is not for me." That is a prideful statement. It is as if to say, "God, I trust my feelings more than I trust You. I trust what I see more than I trust You." I once was like that. I was immature in my faith.

However, God worked with me patiently and once I got a revelation of God's character, I believed in His word. A scripture says that God magnifies His word above His name (see Psalm 138:2).

Since we know how great God's name is, we know His word is even more so. Jesus is the
living Word of God so when we magnify God's word in our lives, we are magnifying the Lord Jesus!

The final phrase that stands out to me in this Psalm is "according to your word." In this phrase, the Psalmist is asking God for something that he needs and states that he asks according to God's own word. Here are some things for which the Psalmist asks:

- To cleanse His way
- Revival
- Strength
- Salvation
- Mercy
- Merciful kindness
- Upholding
- Deliverance
- Understanding

All of these benefits are available to you through prayer. But how do you know what to ask for in prayer unless you know what God's word says? So many people miss out on the abundant life that Jesus died to give us because they do not take time to see what
God's word has to say.

Jesus makes the most amazing promise to us in John 15:7

> "If you abide in Me, and My words abide in you, you will ask what you desire, and it shall be done for you."

Abide means to live in. To live in Jesus means to fellowship with Him, enjoying His presence, studying His word diligently and then ordering your daily decisions according to God's word. When you do that, you gain strong confidence and doubt cannot overtake you.

Fearful

Psalm 56

Focus Scripture: Whenever I am afraid, I will trust in You (Psalm 56:3).

Remember the story of how David defeated Goliath of the Philistines (see 1 Samuel 17)? A few years later, the Philistines captured David and he wrote about his fear of being in the enemy's hands. However, he chose not to give into his fear but put his trust in the Lord instead.

David knew that his trust was not misplaced: "Whenever I am afraid, I will trust in You. In God (I will praise His word), In God I have put my trust; I will not fear. What can flesh do to me?"

Now someone in David's situation might have said, "Well, the Philistines can hurt you and they can kill you."

But Jesus taught his disciples the proper mindset: "And do not fear those who kill the body but cannot kill the soul. But rather fear Him who is able to destroy both soul and body in hell. Are not two sparrows sold for a copper coin? And not one of them falls to the ground apart from your Father's will. But the very hairs of your head are all numbered. Do not fear therefore; you are of more value than many sparrows (Matthew 10:28-31)."

Nothing happens to you without the Lord's knowledge. Because you are valuable to Him, you have no need to fear what man can do to you. Like David, you are confident that
whatever happens is in the Lord's hands.

This scripture also reminds me of Psalm 91:1-2, "He who dwells in the secret place of the Most

High Shall abide under the shadow of the Almighty. I will say of the Lord, 'He is my refuge and my fortress; My God, in Him I will trust.'"

Check your positioning when you are afraid. Are you abiding under the shadow of the Almighty? Make the Lord your hiding place. Scripture tells us that God's perfect love casts out fear. The Lord does not want any of His children living in fear of man nor circumstances.

Because you are secure in God's love, you know He will answer you and at the sound of His voice, the enemy has to flee. So whenever you are afraid, put your trust in the Lord and ensure that you are positioned under His shadow, in the will He has for you. There is no safer place to be than the center of God's will!

Psalm 91

Focus Scripture: "He shall call upon Me, and I will answer him; I will be with him in trouble; I will deliver him and honor him (Psalm 91:15)."

In the United States, we dial '911' whenever an emergency exists and we need immediate aid. So I think of Psalm 91:1 whenever I need God's reassurance that He will be with me in time of trouble!

This Psalm tells me that God keeps me safe in His presence. I can have confidence that He is with me no matter what I go through. It talks about there being a secret place of the Most High. This means a secret place within your heart where you allow the Lord full access so that you can commune with Him in private.

This secret place is the equivalent of the Holy of Holies in the ancient temple. Only the High Priest was allowed to enter in that Holy Place where God's presence dwelled. It was just that priest and the Lord. It was place of quiet, a place of refuge from the turmoil outside as the priest interceded on behalf of the people.

The only limitation to that system was that the priest could only go into the Holy of Holies once per year. But since Jesus came, we can go into the Holy of Holies any time we want.

No matter what is going on in the world, we can always withdraw to a place of quiet and stillness to experience the Lord's presence and hear His voice. What a privilege and honor it is to be able to fellowship with the Most High God!

The Psalm goes on to express the ways in which the Lord will deliver you from trouble when you call upon Him: He delivers you from snares, from pestilence (disease), arrows, destruction. How does God deliver you?

I think one of the most common ways is through His wisdom. He orders your footsteps when you spend time with Him and hear His voice. Have you ever heard His still small voice telling you to go a different way to work or do something that didn't make sense to you at the time, only to find out later that if you had disobeyed, you might have been caught up in an accident or delay?

You never know what trouble you can avoid if only you spend time in the Lord's secret place so that you can hear from Him, become more sensitive to His voice and let Him guide you.

We are also promised protection in the form of angels (see Hebrews 1:13-14). The word says that they shall bear you up. So angels can strengthen and protect us so that we can get on with the Lord's business. To me, it is like an ambassador on business in a hostile, foreign country.

Because the ambassador is valuable to the government of his country, then they assign protection to keep him from injury so that he can do what he has been assigned to do.

God has truly given us everything we need pertaining to life and godliness! In the last few verses, you hear God speaking to the man who has set his love upon him. Setting your love upon God is like making a decision to respond to God's love for you. After all, you love Him because He first loved you. For the man who sets his love upon God, then God says that He sets this man on high, where He is.

Then God makes several promises for them that love Him:

- God will answer when called upon
- God will be with him in trouble

- God will deliver this man and honor him
- God will satisfy this man with long life. So to me, this isn't a long life full of misery. This is a long, satisfied life.
- God will show the man his salvation. Within salvation is safety and security. It means stability and knowing that you don't have to worry.

When you read about these benefits, you can't help but think: "It is good to serve the Lord." Nothing on this Earth compares to what the Lord offers. These benefits are worth far more than silver and gold.

Insecure

Psalm139

---

*Focus Scripture: "You have
hedged me behind and
before, And laid Your hand
upon me.
Such knowledge is too
wonderful for me; It is high,
I cannot attain it (Psalm
139:5- 6).*

Psalm 139 is the perfect antidote when you
are feeling insecure. You may think that
people would not like you if they really
knew you. But the Lord knows you so well
that He even understands your thoughts.
He knows you intimately and loves you
anyway!

David also talks about the Lord's
protection, how the Lord hedges him
from behind and before. To me that
means the Lord redeems

your past, therefore you don't have to replay all of your past mistakes. In Christ Jesus, you are forgiven and He helps you profit from the lessons of the past.

In addition, the Lord hedges you *before*, which means the Lord secures your future. In Jeremiah 29:11, the Lord gives you a promise: "For I know the thoughts that I think toward you, says the Lord, thoughts of peace and not of evil, to give you a future and a hope." Because the Lord has your future in His hands, there is no need to worry about it!

David also talks about the Lord's constant presence in his present. Isn't it comforting to know that the entire Creator of the universe is with you always? In Him is all the wisdom you need to handle every circumstance.

Imagine having an audience with the smartest man on earth. Even that man will look like an idiot compared to God's wisdom!

I also love that David affirms the person that God created him to be. He talks about the Lord forming him and creating his inward parts.

Once you know that God took a personal interest in man's creation, how can you ever think that He would forget about you?

To think that, it would mean that God Himself is like a neglectful landlord; He owns the property, but has no interest in taking care of it. But because you know God then you know that is not true. You can have security in your identity in Jesus Christ, knowing that you belong to Him.

You can also find security in the fact that Jesus has overcome the world! So you can walk forth in all confidence in God, knowing that He will lead you and guide you into the wonderful future that He has for you.

Lonely

Psalm 71

Focus Scripture: "Be my strong refuge, To which I may resort continually; You have given the commandment to save me, For You are my rock and my fortress (Psalm 71:3)."

In the beginning, the first man Adam, had the perfect environment. He had the perfect home (the Garden of Eden), he had a job (naming the animals and tending the Garden), and all his needs were taken care of physically. He had no sickness or infirmity. And I imagine he was quite good looking because he was made in the image of God!

However even with all of these blessings, God said that it was not good for man to be alone.

So God solved the problem through creating a companion for Adam that was comparable to him.

We all desire to have relationships with people to whom we can relate, share our hearts, receive encourage from and to whom we can give encouragement. But what happens when you feel as people have forsaken you, even seek to harm you?

I am sure you agree that it would be hard to find rest and peace in such a situation, never mind praising God. But that's exactly what was happening to the Psalmist here.

He wrote that He will still trust in the Lord, even in the midst of his negative situation. He was counting on the Lord to deliver him and to be his strong refuge.

A place of refuge is generally a place of protection from danger. You need a place of comfort and rest, a place where you can catch your breath and find strength. That is what the Psalmist was counting on the Lord to provide for him. Why did he trust in the Lord to provide this place for him?

The Psalmist concluded that the Lord's character traits make Him the ideal place for refuge. He called the Lord his rock. Solid rock is immovable. Think of the mountains and how majestic they are. If a storm rages around a mountain, that mountain will not move one inch. The Psalmist took comfort that in knowing that the Lord never leaves nor forsakes you and He does not change.

The writer of this Psalm also calls the Lord his fortress. Think about pictures of old medieval castles from the Middle Ages. The fortresses were made out of heavy stones and stacked one on top of the other to build a solid structure. So a fortress had the same protective characteristics as a rock, but was designed as a dwelling place.

So how does one make his dwelling place with the Lord? You can do this through seeking the Lord's presence. He promised in His word that if you seek Him, you will find Him when you seek Him with all of your heart (Deuteronomy 4:29).

Another way that you can dwell with the Lord is through praise. Scripture promises us that we have the garment of praise for the spirit of heaviness. So rather than wallow in his troubles, the Psalmist recognized that even in the toughest circumstances he had reason to praise the Lord.

The Psalmist was not thinking of himself only. He knew that the Lord's goodness deserves to be declared to other people. If you are lonely, to whom can you declare His goodness? Who needs encouragement and strength? The best way to obtain connection with others is to offer it yourself.

Proverbs 18:24 says, "A man who has friends must himself be friendly, But there is a friend who sticks closer than a brother."

Matthew 7:12 says, "Therefore, whatever you want men to do to you, do also to them, for this is the Law and the Prophets."

These principles advise being friendly and kind to people, not as a calculated motive to get friends, but to bring glory to God. When you do that, you can expect that God's word will come to pass in due season.

Whenever you are feeling lonely, then remind yourself that you are never alone. Do not let your feelings be the final authority. Recognize that the Lord is always with you. Why? Because he said he would be and God does not lie.

Oppressed by sin

Psalm 51

Focus Scripture: Deliver me from the guilt of bloodshed, O God, The God of my salvation, And my tongue shall sing aloud of Your righteousness (Psalm 51:14).

Psalm 51 is a heavy Psalm. It was written after the prophet Nathan called out King David for his sin with Bathsheba (see 2 Samuel 12). David had taken another man's wife to bed and after she had gotten pregnant by him, he arranged to have the man killed on the battlefield. Did you really think that drama like this only happens in the movies?

So the prophet Nathan, sent by the Lord, convicted David of what he had done. The baby that David and Bathsheba had conceived died. When David wrote this Psalm he felt that he was oppressed by his sin.

David asked the Lord to have mercy upon him, reminding the Lord of his character of mercy and of lovingkindness. He asked for washing and cleansing because sin makes you feel unclean.

Imagine if you were invited to the White House, but you showed up on the threshold with a dirty body and wearing filthy rags. You would probably feel ashamed that you could not present yourself clean before the president.

That's probably just a fraction of what David felt in the presence of the Lord!

David knew of the Lord's Majesty and splendor. Scripture says that David was a man after God's own heart. David sought to know

God's heart. But based upon his actions with Bathsheba, he did not always do those things that pleased God's heart.

Because David valued his relationship with God, you can imagine the anguish that he felt in knowing that he had done something to impact that relationship for the worse. So he was seeking after restoration and forgiveness.

In verse 4, I always thought it strange that David said that it was only against the Lord that he sinned. He certainly sinned against Bathsheba's husband. After all, he had the man killed! But Bathsheba's husband was one of the Lord's creations, so ultimately it was a sin against the Lord.

David described the feelings from sin's oppression as like having his bones broken. David asked the Lord to hide His face from his iniquities and blot out his transgressions. He also asked the Lord to create a clean heart in him and renew a steadfast spirit within him.

Many people want the Lord to forgive them of past sins, thinking they can keep on sinning because they believe the Lord will forgive them. But that is presumptuous.

We should never ask for the Lord's forgiveness and cleansing with the intention of using God's grace to enable us to continue in sin.

Romans 2:4 asks a pointed question: "Or do you despise the riches of His goodness, forbearance, and longsuffering, not knowing that the goodness of God leads you to repentance?"

Like a father chastises his son, so we should expect that the Lord will discipline us when we do wrong. He doesn't do it for His own amusement; rather He does it to help us see the error of our ways and to lead us back to the right path. He does it because He loves and cares for us.

Through this situation, David learned that obedience to the Lord is better than sacrifice. The Lord is righteous and His word is righteous. Let us be diligent in hiding His word in own hearts and obeying it so that we may not sin against Him.

Psalm 32

Focus Scripture: "Blessed is he whose transgression is forgiven, whose sin is covered (Psalm 32:1)."

What joy to know that our sins are forgiven in Jesus Christ! He paid off our sin debt in full.

Through Him, we have peace with God. In this Psalm, David called the man blessed who sin is forgiven and of whom iniquity is not imputed.

God empowers us to go forth in freedom. Sin no longer has dominion over us for we are not under law, but under grace. Hallelujah! David also says that the man is blessed in whose spirit is not found deceit.

When you try to deceive and hide your sins, the only person you are fooling is yourself ultimately. You don't fool God. After all, He knows everything.

Luke 8:17 says, "For nothing is secret that will not be revealed, nor anything hidden that will not be known and come to light."

So you might as well be honest with God and present your sins to Him for cleansing and forgiveness.

In verse 5, David gives you his experience as he talked with the Lord: "I acknowledged my sin to You, And my iniquity I have not hidden. I said, 'I will confess my transgressions to the

Lord,' And You forgave the iniquity of my sin. Selah."

But that is not all a relationship with God gives you. God gives you His word to hide in your
heart. He says in verse 32:8, "I will instruct you and teach you in the way you should go; I will guide you with My eye."

I have experienced this personally. I used to engage in gluttony regularly. The word the Lord gave to teach me was 1 Corinthians 6:12: "All things are lawful for me, but all things are not helpful. All things are lawful for me, but I will not be brought under the power of any."

God did not set you free from sin so that you can return to sin's bondage. So make it a top priority to seek Him for a word through which you can be free. Proverbs 25:28 says "Whoever has no rule over his own spirit is like a city broken down, without walls."

You do not want to allow any evil thing to come within and destroy you. You've got too much work to do to help build God's kingdom!

So stay mindful of the thoughts you are using to enable yourself to do the wrong thing – and take those thoughts captive to the obedience of Christ. Remind yourself of the word you have hidden in your heart consistently.

In time, you will replace the sin-enabling thought with a grace-empowering thought. With your freedom over sin, you will be glad in the Lord and shout for joy!

Resentful

Psalm 94

Focus Scripture: "If the Lord had not been my help, My soul would soon have dwelt in the abode of silence. If I should say, "My foot has slipped," Your lovingkindness, O Lord, will hold me up (Psalm 94:17-18)."

In this Psalm, the writer is weary because he is seeing his enemies still doing evil and exulting themselves against the Lord, yet nothing seems to change. So the writer is crying out for the Lord to do something!

I once read a story about a drug dealer in Mexico who was on the run from police. He had to move from place to place, only staying in some places for as little as a few hours before he moved somewhere else to avoid capture.

In the end, he was found in a cave with the spaces less than 2 feet wide in spots. They found him with some alcohol and a few survival items. Can you imagine such a life?

And yet, there are probably people who saw him when he had the trappings of wealth and thought he was doing good. That is why we must be careful in comparing our situation to someone else's. We do not know what that person is dealing with.

That drug dealer was brought pretty low. He will likely face a lifetime in jail. He will miss out on the affection of his children and seeing them grow up. And for what? Loving money to the exclusion of loving his fellow man.

What a sad way to live. It is a foolish way to live. This man lost his life because he prioritized the wrong thing and ordered his life according to that wrong thing.

The Psalmist begins his writing by making a case to the Lord as to why the Lord should bring recompense to the wicked. He says that they do their wickedness and think the Lord does not see nor is He paying any attention.

Then the writer addresses the wicked themselves. He calls them senseless and stupid. That is the only conclusion you can come to when you hear about the drug dealer's story!

When I hear about a criminal mastermind getting caught, I think to myself, "The Lord gave you the ability to plan, strategize, think, and come up with creative solutions. And you use that same ability to hurt the ones the Lord loves?"

It is like receiving a precious gift and then turning around to spit in the Lord's face.

But God hears, He sees, He knows, He rebukes. The Lord knows our every thought even before we think it. So in the end, the Lord will bring vengeance upon the wicked. The Psalmist reassures us that the Lord brings us relief until the wicked are brought to justice. The Lord Himself will stand up for us.

The Psalmist ends by writing about how the Lord has been his help, upheld him to keep him from stumbling, comforted his anxious thoughts, been his stronghold and refuge.

We are comforted in the fact that the Lord will bring justice. We only know part of the story but the Lord know the whole story. So we wait patiently for His deliverance which will surely come!

Comfortless

Psalm 77

Focus Scripture: "And I said, 'This is my anguish; But I will remember the years of the right hand of the Most High.' I will remember the works of the Lord; Surely I will remember Your wonders of old (Psalm 77:10)."

Psalm 77 is a Psalm of Asaph and it is about needing comfort in times of trouble. In crying out to the Lord, he expresses his doubt:

- Will the Lord reject forever?
- Will He never be favorable again?
- Has His lovingkindness ceased forever?

- Has His promise come to an end forever?
- Has God forgotten to be gracious?
- Has He withdrawn His compassion in anger?

After asking these questions, I love how the Psalmist gives himself a reality check: "Then I said, 'It is my grief, That the right hand of the Most High has changed.' So the writer reminds himself that the Lord has not changed. He realizes that it is his circumstances that have changed. In his grief, he distorted the Lord's character in his own mind.

What happened to him can happen to us; our emotions can distort reality in our own mind.

Depending on the "emotional glasses" we put on, they can color our world. If we put on glasses with dark colors, everything looks darker. But if we put on light colored glasses, we see the world through the prism of light.

That is why the Bible says in Philippians 4:8, "Finally, brethren, whatever things are true, whatever things are noble, whatever things are just, whatever things are pure, whatever things are lovely, whatever things are of good report, if there is any virtue and if there is anything praiseworthy—meditate on these things."

These are all characteristics of our Lord and Savior! So when we put on these glasses, we can begin to see the world the way that He sees it.

Ephesians 5:8-14 exhorts us: "For you were once darkness, but now you are light in the Lord. Walk as children of light (for the fruit of the Spirit is in all goodness, righteousness, and truth), finding out what is acceptable to the Lord. And have no fellowship with the unfruitful works of darkness, but rather expose them. For it is shameful even to speak of those things which are done by them in secret. But all things that are exposed are made manifest by the light, for whatever makes manifest is light. Therefore He says: 'Awake, you who sleep, Arise from the dead, And Christ will give you light.'"

Instead of continuing to focus on himself, his circumstance, or other people, the Psalmist started focusing on God's greatness. That is awesome pattern for us to follow. We can immediately put on our light glasses through focusing on Jesus, the author and finisher of our faith. After a few minutes of thinking about Jesus and how good He has been to you, then check your emotions.

If you feel greater peace, joy, and/or love then you know you are back in the light.

Praise the Lord for helping us to walk in the light as He is in the light!

Psalm 61

Focus Scripture: "Hear my cry, O God; Attend to my prayer. From the end of the earth I will cry to You, When my heart is overwhelmed; Lead me to the rock that is higher than I (Psalm 61:1-2)."

Psalm 61 is about God's protection when your heart is in distress. Let's face it; life can be hard! You experience loss or lack. Somebody hurts your feelings. Things don't turn out as you expected. People disappoint you. A loved one dies. Someone you care about makes unwise decisions that hurt them.

During those hard times, cry out to God! Jesus gave you a Comforter. A Comforter is one who soothes your soul, your mind, will and emotions in times of distress. In our faith, the Holy Spirit is the one who comforts. The

Psalmist says that he cries out to God in prayer no matter where he is.

When you are overwhelmed, your heart feels unstable, as if you are in danger of your emotions sweeping you away. So the Psalmist prays: "Lead me to the rock that is higher than I."

Seeking stability is a good strategy when dealing with an emotional problem. You need to seek a vantage point that is higher than the problem. A practical way to do that is to magnify the Lord above your problem.

As you meditate upon God's greatness, character and deeds, and you know the Lord is on your side, then suddenly there is confidence and peace. Suddenly, you realize that God is ready and willing to help you with whatever comes your way. That is a priceless feeling.

The Psalmist also reminds himself of what God has been to him in the past: God has been a shelter for him and a strong tower from the enemy. So because God has been there for him in the past, then he tells himself that he is going to abide (live) in the tabernacle forever and trust in the shelter of God's wings.

Both of these are personal decisions each of us must make. You see, the Psalmist is not questioning whether he is going to continue to follow the Lord or not. He has settled the issue in his mind and heart.

So many people stay with the Lord when times are good, but start seeking answers elsewhere during challenging times. However, that is the wrong thing to do.

Who knows more about life issues than God? Who knows all about your past, present, and future? God. Who loves you more? God. And because He loves you, who is going to give you

the perfect answer for your situation?
God. In light of that, who is the One to call
on? God!

God hears our prayers and He has a
heritage for those of us who fear Him. We
have eternal life! It is our heritage to know
God's character in fellowship with Him. His
mercy and truth preserve us. He is our
inheritance and portion forever. He is our
Savior. He is our strength, He is our
protector.

We praise the Lord for waking us up in
the morning, and for starting us on our
way. He causes His face to shine upon
us and is gracious to us. He gives us
peace and joy.

God doesn't just send us off for the day like a
mother might send her child off to school.
Nope, he stays with us all day! His grace
covers us wherever we go. That is a
wonderful fact in which to take comfort.

The Positive Emotions

In these final Psalm chapters, I decided to add a few positive ones. I didn't want you to think that the book of Psalm focused only on negative emotions. Far from it!

Most of the Psalm are written as praises to God. So in that spirit, let's exalt His name together!

Grateful

Psalm 40

"'Let all those who seek You rejoice and be glad in You; Let such as love Your salvation say continually, "The Lord be magnified! (Psalm 40:15)"

A psychiatrist once said that people who suffer from neurotic disorders, such as depression or anxiety, almost always have a habit of fault finding. They focus on faults within themselves or faults with other people. No matter what else was good in their lives, they always focused on what was wrong and lacking.

When I suffered from depression years ago, I was like that. But I discovered a simple key that could change my mental state instantly. In Psalm 40, the writer uses this key: Gratitude.

My husband and I had a conversation recently about how easy it is to fall into complaining and negativity. Why? Because it feels good to the flesh to indulge in it.

However, those thoughts and words are leading you somewhere. If you don't like where you are, then you need to retrace the steps that got you there.

So a wise thing to do is always ask yourself where your words and thoughts are leading you. Are they leading you to quit on a goal? Dissatisfaction with your mate or your life in general? Are they leading to distance between yourself and other people?

You might say that this sounds like a lot of work to change your thoughts and words. It is. But it is work worth doing. Think about it: Do you really want to get to the end of your life full of regrets over what might have been?

Most of our errors in life can be traced back to our thoughts and words, which led to wrong actions, habits, and the results we are now experiencing. It is the law of sowing and reaping in action.

We can't plant bad seeds and then expect a good harvest. Sowing seeds of gratitude will lead to a good harvest!

Even in the midst of trials, the Psalmist doesn't lose sight of all the things the Lord has done for him. He expresses gratitude that the Lord heard his prayer, that He delivered him, gave him stability, and that the Lord established his steps.

The Psalmist even says that the Lord gave him a new song in his mouth. Imagine being able to sing in the midst of trouble. It may seem impossible to some but with the Lord all things are possible. One of the purposes of our being able to sing in the midst of trials is that it gives a powerful testimony to others that having the all-powerful God on our side makes a difference.

God's vision for His people is that we stand out from the world, not blend in. The Psalmist says that he will declare the Lord's righteousness, faithfulness, and salvation in the assembly. In spite of his troubles, the writer encourages others to rejoice and be glad. Even though the writer says that he is poor and needy, he affirms that the Lord is his help.

Meditating in your heart about that for which you are grateful and praising God at all times helps ensure He is present in your circumstances. When the Lord is on the scene, you can have confidence that He is working it out!

Happy

Psalm 92

Focus Scripture: "It is good to give thanks to the Lord, And to sing praises to Your name, O Most High; To declare Your lovingkindness in the morning, And Your faithfulness every night (Psalm 92: 1-2)

There was a song called "Happy" a few years ago that was very popular. The singer created the world's first 24-hour video that featured different segments with the song playing, but different people dancing to the tune. It made me smile to see the video because you had people of all races, ages, genders, sizes - all dancing and lip syncing to the 'Happy' song.

In Psalm 92, the writer is clearly in a happy state. Even though he wrote this message thousands of years ago, all of us who trust in the Lord can dance to the same tune!

The Psalmist says that the reason we can be happy is that we have reasons to praise the Lord morning and night; we can praise Him in the morning for His lovingkindness. We can praise Him for His faithfulness every night.

In the morning, I am thankful to the Lord sending His Son Jesus to save me from my sins. Scripture says that God so loved the world that He gave His only begotten son, that whoever

believes in Him shall not perish but
has everlasting life (John 3:16).

It astonishes me that God did this for us.
He could have just left mankind to perish
in our sins, but He didn't. He sent Jesus
because He knew that we could not save
ourselves.
Without Jesus, there was no way a sinful
people could have a relationship with a
Holy God. So His love for us and His
kindness toward us is a reason to rejoice.

You can praise God at night for His
faithfulness. After you look back on your
day, you can see
God's handiwork and recognize that it was
only because of His protection, presence,
and provision that you were able to make it.

The writer talks about making music with
various instruments. He is glad in
celebrating the work of the Lord's hands.
We are the Lord's workmanship too and
we were created for good works.

When we operate in the Lord's excellence, then others will see our good works and it will inspire them to glorify God. That is the purpose of our life - to glorify God in body and Spirit.

One of the things that I like to do is keep a journal to write down all the blessings that the Lord has imparted to me. Otherwise, it is too easy to forget. The Psalmist talks about seeing the Lord's desire upon His enemies, allowing the writer to triumph. You can see the victory as he writes about it and the satisfaction and peace that comes with it.

He finishes the writing by specifying the rewards that are available to those whose hope is in God. He says that we will like palms trees and cedar trees. A palm tree is flexible, able to withstand hurricane-force winds. A cedar tree is also strong, but is able to remain planted, not uprooted. Staying planted in the Lord means that you have your roots in Him.

The Psalmist says that those in the Lord shall flourish. That means that we shall experience abundance in every area. This doesn't mean that we just survive, but thrive. Our lives look different from the world - better because of the God we serve. And because our association with the Lord is evident then it makes people curious as to the reason for our hope. Then we are able to tell them about Jesus, who is the author and finisher of our faith.

That is the bottom line. Prosperity is good but the ultimate reason for us to prosper is not just for us. It is a testimony to others about how good it is to serve the Lord so that they can taste and see that the Lord is good for themselves.

That is what I want for my family and friends. So I press into my God and am happy because of what He has done, what He is doing, and in anticipation for what He is going to do!

Psalm 66

In Psalm 66, the writer's emotion is best described as exultation. Not only is he celebrating God's goodness, but he wants other people to join in!

His message is not to be quiet about what the Lord has done for you, but to make some noise. He exhorts the people to shout and sing. Most importantly of all, he asks the people to speak to the Lord Himself about His greatness.
He affirms the Lord's works are worthy of praise. He celebrates the Lord's great, awesome, and wonderful name.

In the next paragraph, he invites the people to review how God has shown Himself strong in their lives. In this particular instance, since he is speaking to the nation of Israel, he is reviewing what the Lord has done in their history. He talks about God's miracle of drying up the sea so that they could cross. In this great miracle, God brought the Israelites out of slavery in Egypt into freedom in the Promised Land.

God also brought us from slavery into freedom. We were enslaved to sin and didn't even know it. We did things the way the world did them and experienced the same results that the world did. The wages of sin is death. So when we engaged in sin then we experienced death in some way.

We might have experienced death in a relationship, in our future wealth because we spent our money on frivolous things, we might have experience death in our health as we spent our time on worthless habits, only later in life to discover that we missed out on the vitality of youth because of our choices.

But God saved us from death. Through Jesus Christ, we have newness of life! We rejoice in our new freedom and marvel at the Lord's power. Of all the miracles God performs, the greatest is His capacity to transform the human heart! He is amazing, but so loving and gentle to those He calls His own.

Not only has the Lord shown Himself mighty in our past but He continues to do so in our present. He is the Alpha and the Omega, the beginning and the end. It is all about Him. He protects us daily and keeps us steady.

Scripture says that the steps of a good man are ordered by the Lord and He delights in his way (Psalm 37:23). So when we follow in the path that God sets for us, we bring delight to the Lord. T

In the next passage, the writer discusses the history of Israel's rebellion. The Lord had told the Israelites if they follow Him, He would dwell among them but if they didn't then He would remove the protection from them and allow their enemies to overtake them. The people did not listen and the Lord heeded His own word. The people experienced much affliction because of their disobedience.

However, the writer also says that God used the experience to refine them as silver is refined. When you refine silver, you remove the dross, which is worthless. The more of the dross you remove, the clearer and purer the silver becomes. It increases in value.

Plus, the purer the silver becomes the more reflective it becomes. We can't reflect the greatness of our God if we are full of dross! We want people to experience the fullness of God so we must reflect the fullness of God ourselves.

Finally, the writer invites others to hear about what the Lord has done for him. Because he is meditating on the goodness of God, then that leads Him to repentance. When you meditate on God's goodness, you naturally draw closer to Him.

The Lord longs to hear from us and has promised that when we pray according to His will and word, He hears us. And if He hears us, then we have the petitions we have asked of Him.

My soul cries out Hallelujah because He has truly given us everything that we need. Best of all, He has given us His joy and peace so that we can enjoy all of His blessings.

Conclusion

The goal of learning to manage your emotions God's way is so that you can reflect His character accurately to a world that needs Him desperately. You can do that when you allow the Holy Spirit to lead you to the truth.

Why is truth so important? Because if you are living according to lies, then you will make errors in judgement that lead you to ultimate failure. The biggest failure of all is refusing to accept life in Jesus Christ. As a Believer in Jesus, our mandate is to lead as many people to life in Him as we can.

The world is supposed to see Jesus in us. We are being transformed into the image of Christ from glory to glory.

Aren't you glad that even when your emotions threaten to overwhelm you, you can find hope and strength in God's word? From that dark place, all you have to do is seek it out. It is your lifeline.

When you do that, you can lead others into the light of God's love.

Jesus said that His words are Spirit and they are life. Do you want more life? Then create a treasury of Jesus' words in your heart.

Thank you Jesus for your love and for Your word that heals us!

About the Author

Kimberly Taylor is the creator of **Takebackyourtemple.com**, a website that inspires Christians to Spiritual, emotional, and physical health. She is the author of the ebook *Take Back Your Temple* and the books *The Weight Loss scriptures, God's Word is Food*, and **many others**.

Once 240 pounds and a size 22, Kim lost 85 pounds through renewing her mind and taking action upon God's word. Her experience led her to establish the **Take Back Your Temple** website. "Take Back Your Temple" is a prayer that asks God to take control of your body and your life so He can use them for His purpose and agenda.

Kim's weight loss success story has been featured on CBN's *The 700 Club,* and in *Prevention Magazine*, *Essence Magazine*, *Charisma Magazine* and many other magazines and newspapers. She has also been interviewed on various radio programs.

Kim exhorts people of faith to become good stewards of all the resources God has given to them, including time, money, talents, and physical health. "I am passionate about empowering others to adopt healthy lifestyles so they can fulfill their God-given purpose," she says.

"My dream is for God's people to stand apart because we are healthy, prosperous and living the abundant life to which we are called. I want non-believers to look at us and want what we have: Spiritual, mental, and physical wholeness. Then when they ask us what we are doing differently, we can tell them about Jesus, the author and finisher of our faith."

Made in the USA
Thornton, CO
11/21/23 15:42:49

baecd0e5-3576-40c5-b178-a377506b2f42R02